THE POST PA HANDBOOK

ALYSSA CARROLL

THE POST PA HANDBOOK

YOUR GUIDE TO LIFE AS A POST PRODUCTION ASSISTANT IN TELEVISION AND MOVIES

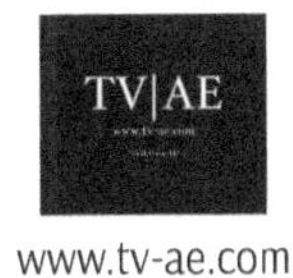

www.tv-ae.com

CONTENTS

CONTENTS

INTRODUCTION

My name is Alyssa Carroll. I'm a television editor and the creator of TV-AE.com. In the beginning of my career I was a post production assistant for shows on the networks ABC, NBC, AMC, The CW, and more. I love research, and when I was starting out I found myself yearning for detailed information about how to be a good post production assistant. I found a lot of on-set guides but nothing for my specific career path. So, after a decade in the industry, I decided to write my own guide. This handbook is for people like me who love information and want to do their best work. If you'd like to learn more about my professional credits, you can find me on IMDb here: https://imdb.me/alyssa-carroll.

A Note on This Book

My experience is grounded in Los Angeles, California, where I began my post production career. Therefore, most of my examples will be from a Los Angeles viewpoint, and most of my advice is from an American perspective. That being said, there are lots of practical pieces of information in this handbook for any location, and this handbook will be helpful to most people in the early stages of their post production career.

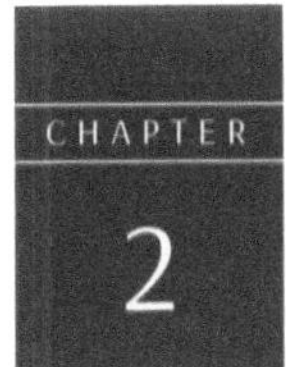

WELCOME TO THE INDUSTRY

Congratulations! You graduated from film school or you decided to take the leap and move out to Los Angeles, New York, Atlanta, or another film and television hub. You have dreams of becoming an editor or the Head of Post Production at a major studio. Now, it's time to find your first job. But where do you begin?

In the field of post production, you begin as a post production assistant.

WHAT IS A POST PRODUCTION ASSISTANT?

A post production assistant or editorial assistant, colloquially known as a post PA, supports the editorial team on a film or television show. They support the editor, assistant editor, post producer, post supervisor, and post coordinator. A post PA's duties may include:

- Getting meals and coffee for the team.
- Delivering hard drives or other physical deliverables to various departments.
- Keeping all written information up-to-date, like schedules, contact lists, and meeting notes.
- Answering phones.
- Taking notes in screenings, meetings, and note sessions.
- Helping to schedule ADR* sessions.
- Printing and distributing paperwork.

· Keeping track of petty cash and receipts.

Post production assistants are the first step into the world of post production and a vital part of any production.

***DEFINITION:** ADR is short for Automated (Or Additional) Dialogue Replacement. It refers to re-recording dialogue audio in a controlled setting to improve the audio quality or reflect a change in performance or word choice. You may also hear ADR referred to as "looping."

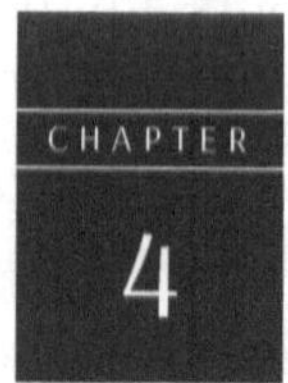

DO I NEED TO MOVE TO LOS ANGELES?

You can create a film career for yourself anywhere in the world, but you will learn a lot more if you're in a major city for the first few years of your career. So, I suggest doing at least two years in a production hub like Los Angeles, California, or New York, New York.

Los Angeles and New York are not the end-all-be-all of the industry. There is post production work for film and television in other locations such as Chicago, IL, Atlanta, GA, Boston, MA and more. In addition, there is post production work in public broadcasting, commercials, and social media in almost any major city in the United States. You can also work abroad in places like Canada, England, or Australia. If you're multi-lingual, there is a film industry in most countries. Wherever you want to live, there are options for you. However, the vast majority of film or television work will be in the cities of Los

Angeles or New York. Your connections in those cities will serve you well if you ever decide to move away.

Moving to a new city can be temporary, and leaving a city is not a failure. Find what works best for you.

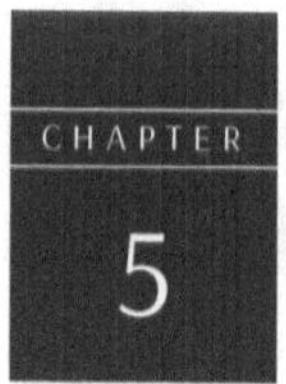

SHOULD I TAKE AN INTERNSHIP?

Internships are worthwhile. I firmly believe that internships are a great way to make connections that last throughout your career. They're also a great way to get your foot in the door. Just remember - internships are about learning. As a post production assistant, you are paid to get coffee. As an intern, you are paid less than a PA and you still have to get coffee, but you are also given the opportunity to sit in with the editor, the assistant editor, the post producer, and anyone else in the cutting room to learn if their career path is the right career path for you. As an intern, ask for learning opportunities and take them seriously when offered.

Paid internships are becoming easier to find. Thankfully, most companies have woken up to the fact that only those who have the means to survive while unemployed can take an unpaid internship. It simply isn't an option for most of us.

So, ask for compensation if you find a company that wants to offer you an internship. You do not need to work for free.

One internship that is well worth your time and energy is the American Cinema Editors (ACE) Internship. They're not a sponsor of this handbook. I just like the program. The application fee may feel steep, but as part of the application you get tickets to a lecture series that is absolutely worth the price. In addition, you get an opportunity to meet other people in the field and to learn from experienced assistant editors and editors. I cannot recommend this program enough if you need more contacts in Hollywood.

You can find the application on their website: https://americancinemaeditors.org/

FINDING WORK

Getting that first job is hard, and people don't acknowledge how hard it truly is. It's a chicken and an egg problem. Companies want people with experience, but you can only get experience if a company accepts you without experience. It's exhausting! However, don't give up because it's hard. There are lots of people who are willing to give a new person a chance. Plus, you're strong. You can do this.

The perfect job for you could be right around the corner. Make sure you're prepared. Have your resume ready. Have a template for your cover letter so you can quickly type in the relevant information. Ensure you have asked your references if they are okay with representing you and if it's okay to share their contact information. I'll break down each of these steps in the following pages.

Once you're ready, you can start applying for jobs.

Professional Headshots

I suggest getting a professional headshot taken.

We are not actors, so you might find this suggestion odd, but I would suggest this for any working professional. Of course, you should not put your picture on your resume. However, you'll want a picture of yourself for your LinkedIn profile and maybe even your IMDb page.

Hire a professional, not a friend. Photographers who do headshots for a living are excellent resources. They know how to make you look relaxed, professional, hire-able, yet fun. Most headshot photographers provide hairstyling and make-up in their packages, and some even help you pick the best outfit.

I vividly remember applying to my first job, and the interviewer asked for a photo of me so he could find me at the coffee shop where we were going to meet for the interview. I had nothing professional-looking to send him, and I spent the next hour putting together a professional-looking outfit and forcing a friend to take pictures of me. It was a stress I did not want, which I could have avoided if I had a picture on file that I could easily attach to an email. My friend's photo was nowhere near as good as the professional headshot I got a few years later. It's worth the time and money to get a headshot taken professionally.

The Resume

Resumes should be one page. You may already have a CV from prior experience. A CV has a variable length and provides a detailed overview of your education or career. In film and television, you must provide a resume. A resume is a bite-sized look at your career. When people ask for your resume, they want an easy-to-digest summary of your most relevant experience and skills. Resumes should always be one page.

Your resume needs to be readable. Most experts say your resume should be so clear that artificial intelligence can easily read it. You are a creative person, and you want to stand out. I completely understand that. However, this is not the time to be overly creative. Your resume needs to have predictable fonts and precise wording. That doesn't mean your resume needs to be boring, but clarity needs to be your top priority. A pop of color is good, but remember that somebody might print your resume in greyscale. Test your resume in greyscale to make sure it's legible. Send your resume to five trusted people before sending it to a potential employer. Ask those trusted people for feedback, and adjust your resume as needed.

Your resume should not include your photograph. However, you can have a small graphic of your own design if graphic design is something you want to showcase.

RESUME BASICS

Every resume should include the following:

- Your first and last name
- Your email and phone number
- Your education
- Your work experience
- Relevant skills
- A reference

First and Last Name

If you prefer a screen name or nickname, you can put that name on your resume instead of your legal name. Just be sure to give the accounting department your legal name when you are hired.

If you do not want to use a screen name or nickname, put your legal name here. Middle names are not required.

Education

Most people want to give alums from their alma mater a step up. So, be sure to put your college or university on your resume.

Not everyone in the film industry has a college degree. If you do not have a college degree, then be sure to put your highest level of education on your resume, like your high school degree or GED completion. In addition, if you have any extra accreditations or certificates, put those in this section. For instance, you might be Avid Media Composer certified.

Work Experience

Something I hear a lot from recent graduates is: "I don't have any experience." And I'm here to tell you that's not true. You already have a lot of experience. Were you an officer for a club in college or high school? Put it on your resume. Did you edit every music video for an up-and-coming musician? Put it on your resume. Did you volunteer your time and energy with a non-profit organization? Put it on your resume. Are you the best darn babysitter this side of the Mississippi? Put it on your resume! You have more experience than you might think.

Early-career resumes should show commitment, punctuality, and an ability to learn and adapt. You need to show how your job at the mall or long-time participation at an organization translates into you being a dependable hire.

If you are a veteran, be sure to put that here as well. A few studios have specific programs to help veterans get placed in film industry jobs, and most people see military experience as proof of self-discipline and hard work.

Relevant Skills

As previously stated, this section can feel challenging to fill out, but you probably have more skills than you think. Be sure to list both hard skills and soft skills. Hard skills are job-related technical knowledge, while soft skills refer to interpersonal skills.

First, think about hard skills. What technical knowledge do you have? List software that you're comfortable using. This list could include Zoom, GoogleDrive Suite, Excel, Avid Media Composer, Adobe After Effects, and Adobe Premiere. If you have worked in tech support, then you could include troubleshooting. You can even include skills outside the office realm, like knowing how to drive a car with a manual transmission, 3D printing, basic budgeting, or accounting. I put balloon animals as a skill on my resume because it's a hobby I enjoy and gives interviewers something to talk to me about. I know people who have been hired as a production assistant because they knew how to move the director's car. Make a big list, then cut it down to the most relevant and fun skills.

Next, think about soft skills. What interpersonal skills do you have? Some of those skills may include customer service, time management, punctuality, communication, patience, empathy, teamwork, or a willingness to learn. If you know how to run a meeting, put that in here. Soft skills are much harder to quantify, but you know what you're good at. Take a few minutes to write down the skills you learned in other jobs that you think will translate.

Once you have your extensive list of skills, put five to ten items on your resume. You want to use this section to show that you're qualified while not overwhelming the page with your skills.

References

A reference is a person who can vouch for your work ethic, ability to learn, or your overall character. Choose your references carefully. Your references should be people you are confident will give a glowing review of your work.

Always ask someone before listing them as a reference on your resume. Ask them if they're comfortable sharing their email and phone number. They may only be comfortable sharing their email or want the line "contact information available upon request" on your resume. Respect their wishes.

Sample Resume

Take a look at the sample resume on the next page. What would you change? Is the information as clear as it could be?

Jane Doe

janedoeemail@emails.com
555-555-5555

Education

BFA from
College
University

Skills

Software:
Avid Media
Composer
Adobe Premiere
Adobe After
Effects

Other Skills:
Good
Communicator
Attention to Detail
Punctual

Reference

Name
Title
Email

Work Experience

Tech Support at College University
September 2020 - May 2023 (During
School Year)
Responsible for:
- Helping students troubleshoot
software issues
- Overseeing inventory

Retail Job
May 2022 - September 2022
Responsible for:
- Excellent customer service
- Handling the checkout process
- Processing returns

Child Care
2022 - 2023
5-Star Rated on
BabysittingWebsite.com
Responsible for:
- Night-time routines
- Meal prep and feedings
- Fun and games

The Cover Letter

A good cover letter includes the following:

- Intro paragraph - Who are you? How did you learn about this job? Ask for the job!
- What do you hope to gain in the role - What excites you?
- What background makes you qualified for the position - What is your experience? What makes you unique?
- Summary and Thank You - Attach your resume and references.

Here's an example of a cover letter from someone applying for a post production assistant job on a television show about superheroes:

Example Cover Letter Email

Subject Line: Post PA Application for Superhero Show

Hello James,

My name is Jane Doe. I saw on the "Hire a Post PA" Facebook group that you're seeking a post production assistant for a superhero TV show. I would like to apply for the job. I have attached my resume and references for you.

I would be a good fit for this position because of my successful run as a Post PA on *Fun TV Show* last year. On that show, I learned how to schedule ADR and I implemented a weekly voting system that made lunches more fun and varied. I also have a deep love of superheroes. I went to LA Comic Con last year as Poison Ivy, and I know I'd be a fun addition to an office of superhero fans.

Do you need any other information from me?

I look forward to talking with you.

Sincerely,
Jane Doe
She/Her
(phone number)
(email)

Example Cover Letter Explained

You'll notice a few things about that cover letter.

The subject line of the email clearly states the goal of the email. Please note: Many job posts require specific wording for the subject line. They do this because it's an easy way to weed out applications. Their thought process is: you need to follow the directions they set up in the application to be capable of following their directions on the job. Therefore, use the wording they request.

This cover letter is informal. The letter does not start with "To Whom It May Concern." This position would rarely require submitting your resume to an unnamed entity. More often than not, you're submitting your resume to a real person. It's okay to address them by their first name. Film and television is an informal industry. It is essential to spell the interviewer's name correctly and not assume their gender identity.

Jane lets the potential employer know how she found out about this job. If you received this information from a specific person who has worked with the employer in the past, be sure to include that information in the email.

In the first section, Jane informs the employer that her resume is attached. This has two advantages. 1) It lets the employer know you have provided the relevant information. 2) When you include the word "attached," most email software will stop the email from being sent if nothing is attached. We all make mistakes, and this is a good way of catching one before it goes out to anyone.

Next, you'll notice that there is a bit of bragging. Let the employer know you're qualified by telling them what you learned on your last job, what you were in charge of, and what you improved upon. Give a short but specific story about your skills.

In the second paragraph, you'll notice that Jane Doe showed some personality. She let her employer know about a hobby outside of work. Keep this part relevant to the job posting and reasonably short. However, letting them know you're a real person will help you stick out in their mind. This is also an excellent section to show that you've done some research on the television show or feature film. You can say you were excited by the Variety article, loved the last season, or perhaps that the lead actor is someone you admire. Remember, this is not a fan letter; this is not the time to spend paragraphs gushing about a star.

Near the end, you'll see that Jane ended her email with a question. This prompts the interviewer to reply to you, which helps you know that they received your email and opens the line of communication if needed.

Put your full name, phone number, and email address in the signature. If you use a stage name on your resume, be sure to use the same name in your email signature. I also suggest putting your pronouns. It's not possible to know your gender via email, and I find that people appreciate having the information so they can properly address you.

Remember, be succinct and be polite.

After a few days, it's okay to follow up if you are still waiting for a reply. You can say, "Hi, I just want to make sure you received this email," but let it go if the follow-up doesn't go anywhere.

You will get rejected. That's part of the process. The rejection is not personal, but it could mean you should improve your resume or your cover letter. Have a mentor read over both to make sure you're presenting your information well. There are always more jobs and more opportunities.

Where Do I Look for Work?

Networking

Networking is the number one tool in your toolbox for finding work. Unfortunately, many people hear "networking" and immediately think of people being sleazy and only making connections if it benefits them. That's not at all what I'm suggesting. Instead, make genuine connections, and sustain them. Be interested in the other person and talk to them like a friend. It can help to keep in mind that networking flows both ways and you may be in a position to recommend someone in the future who takes the time to recommend you today. Ultimately, you want to be making friends rather than searching for meal tickets.

It's hard. I find networking to be quite difficult. However, most of the work I have ever gotten has been because of a connection. It's well worth your time to build a supportive community. Here are a few quick tips for making interpersonal connections:

- Be interested in the other person. Ask follow-up questions about their life or job.
- Work on positive body language. Make eye contact. Deliver a firm handshake. Smile and keep your arms uncrossed while speaking and listening.
- Listen! It's great to contribute to the conversation, but make sure your new friend gets time to talk too.

· Keep the trauma in the therapist's office. Share work-appropriate content and keep any anger, dating woes, or overly personal information out of the conversation.

Along with the preceding tips, be sure to stay professional. Many networking events serve alcohol, and it could be all too easy to overimbibe. Remember that you are representing your professional self.

Here are a few other networking suggestions. Send an email to the team that you interned with and say hi. Have you used a skill recently that you picked up at your internship? Let them know. People love hearing that they have helped you grow.

Answer emails you receive.

Go to a book club or wine night with fellow post production assistants. If you can't find one, organize one! Invite people you met at the ACE Internship Lecture Series.

Go to meet-ups hosted by professional organizations like Blue Collar Post Collective or the Editors Guild.

· http://www.bluecollarpostcollective.com/
· https://www.editorsguild.com/

Go for "reach connections," like that person who graduated three years before you who is doing cool stuff now.

Ask your friends what they're doing to network, and join them when they attend events.

Keep going. Keep connecting.

Shadowing

Job shadowing is a type of training that allows an interested person to follow and closely observe another person performing their job. Shadowing is one of my favorite networking tools because it helps you grow your skill set and connects you with someone in your industry.

If a person in your network is doing the type of work you want to do, then ask to shadow that person for a day or even for a couple hours. Most people love showing off their skills and letting people see what they do for a living. When I asked to shadow, I was only turned down once, and it was due to the high level of security surrounding the show. It's worth putting yourself out there to ask.

Be sure to bring a notebook when you shadow. You will learn a vast amount simply by sitting over someone's shoulder, and you don't want to forget it.

On the day of, ask if you can bring in coffee or some fancy donuts to thank them for their time. Then, be sure to send a thank you email afterward. They did not need to take time out of their day. They did it to help you. Be grateful for their time and effort.

Facebook

Facebook Groups are a great place to look for work. I have found that potential employers post there before posting on dedicated job websites. There are Facebook groups dedicated to the film and television industry, and they even get as specific as post production or production assistant job openings. So, Facebook ranks as one of my top places to research open positions.

Here are a few Facebook Groups that I have found to be very useful:

- Assistant Editors in LA - this is specific to Los Angeles, but try a search for your city. I know New York has a similar group.
- Blue Collar Post Collective - they are nationwide and very active. They also hold get-togethers, which are a great way to network.
- I Need a PRODUCTION ASSISTANT! - this group is massive, but it often has good posts if you're looking for last-minute work.
- Post Production/Editing Jobs - this group is worldwide and tends to have a wide range of posts, but sometimes has good job postings.

Join your alumni Facebook Group. A lot of people try to give graduates from their alma mater a step up. Take advantage of that by joining the group for your college or university.

If you are part of a marginalized group, search for Facebook Groups that include your niche and post production or film and television. For example:

· Women in Post Production
· Deaf & Disabled People in TV

Job Websites

https://staffmeup.com/

I hate to suggest a paid site, but this one is worth your investment. You can look for and apply to some jobs without paying, but you'll hit a limit quickly. Many unscripted television shows use Staff Me Up, and they're often looking for staff. Take the time to create a compelling profile, and send a cover letter specific to the job you are applying to.

https://www.mandy.com/

Mandy is another large job posting site for the film and television industry. I find that there is less post production work there than on StaffMeUp, but it's definitely worth taking the time to check it out.

You can also search for job websites that are specific to a region. For example, New York has the Post New York Alliance (https://www.postnewyork.org/) which has a job board for members.

LinkedIn

https://www.linkedin.com/

I have never once found a job on LinkedIn, and I don't know anyone who has. That being said, people look at the profiles a lot. I think of this like my living, long-form resume. It grows with me. Put your professional headshot on your page. If you don't have your headshot yet, choose a work appropriate photo of yourself. Ensure it is just you in the picture, no friends or pets. List all the work experience that you added to your resume. Add connections. If you made a good networking connection at a meet-up, take the time later to add them on LinkedIn.

IMDb

https://www.imdb.com/

There are better places to find work than IMDb, but it's an excellent place for people to find you. Keep this updated in the same way you would update your LinkedIn. Employers will look you up on IMDb, so create a profile ahead of time and put what credits you can on there. You can add credits without an IMDbPro account, but you won't have control over which credit comes up first on your profile without paying.

You can use the paid IMDbPro account to rearrange your credits and feature specific projects. You can also use the secret weapon of the paid pro account - finding contact information. Do you have an editor you admire? Use your pro account to find their agent. Reach out to their agent and ask if you can come into the cutting room and shadow the editor for a day. It's always worth asking! If you get a polite no, take it with grace. Thank the agent for their time, and let them know that you'd be happy to shadow any editor on their roster. The agent might suggest someone else or politely decline again.

Cutting rooms can be busy and tense, and editors might not have the capacity to have visitors. If you get radio silence, remember that agents are very busy. Silence is not automatically a no. You can send one follow-up email if they don't respond within a week. Try to avoid the phrase "just checking in" in your email. Instead, go with something like, "Hi, I want to make sure you saw this email. Would you prefer a quick phone call? My number is: xxx-xxx-xxxx," and see if they'd rather call and talk to you. Two attempts at contact are the limit. If you don't hear back after that, then move on.

Avoid Scams

Unfortunately, there are scams out there. Here are some tell-tale signs of a job scam:

- They don't post a pay rate/scale – California and New York now require employers to post the pay rate, or a general scale for the pay rate, when they post a job. This is excellent news. You won't waste your time applying to non-paying "jobs," and it helps to flag scams. It's a relatively new law, so if someone has not posted the pay rate, please ask for the information. If you get a constant reply of "based on experience," then don't apply.

- They ask you for money or ask you to hold money for them - A widespread scam is one where they ask you to accept a wire transfer or pick up wired money and send it to them. Do not agree to those terms. Legitimate places will not ask you to send them money.
- They refuse to set up an in-person or Zoom interview - if they won't call you, Zoom you, or meet you, then they probably don't exist.

If you need clarification on the validity of a job, check out the IMDb and LinkedIn of the person you're connecting with to see if they have worked on any actual film or television shows. Only send out personal information if you're sure of the recipient.

Every show I have ever worked for has asked for a copy of my passport to verify my identity for payroll. That is very normal. However, you do not need to send it to the employer beforehand. If you need more clarification about a job, let them know you do not feel comfortable emailing a copy of your passport. Tell them you'll happily bring your passport on your first day. After that, if you get a lot of pushback, walking away is okay.

Remember, this opportunity is not your only opportunity.

THE INTERVIEW

Congratulations! You have an interview! Here are a few things to keep in mind:

- Do your research. Watch the show beforehand, or read the Deadline or Variety article if it's a pilot or a first-season show. Watch the director's or the editor's previous work for a feature.
- Be on time. (5 minutes early = on time)
- Don't chew gum, vape, or smoke. Be respectful of their space.
- Relax. An interviewer is just a person, and so are you. Treat it like a friendly conversation.
- Be polite to everyone in the office or at the coffee shop. Your interviewer will likely ask the receptionist how you were or they may know the barista. How you act outside the interview is of interest to the interviewer.

- Don't lie. If you don't know how to do something, let the interviewer know you're willing to learn.
- Have at least one question prepared to ask the interviewer. One of my go-to's is, "What does success in this position look like to you?"
- Ask when you will hear about a decision, but don't demand an exact deadline. The interviewer might know that they need a PA in two weeks, but they might not have an exact date that they are going to hire someone.
- Thank them for their time at the end of the interview. They didn't have to meet with you, so thank them for taking the time out of their day.
- Email them a thank you note when you get home.

Where to Interview

Most shows and films still need their offices, also called cutting rooms, set up before they start looking for staff. This results in a lot of coffee shop interviews. If you have time, visit the coffee shop the day before the interview, which will help you determine information like where to park your car.

If you're in a metropolitan area like New York City that has good public transit, you can take public transit to your interview location. Try to take the journey the day before so you're sure about which train line and which stops bring you to your interview.

If you're one of the lucky few, you might interview on a studio lot. Studio lots require a "Drive-On" or a pass that allows you to enter the lot. Most studios have multiple entrances and exits. To utilize your drive-on, you must enter through a specific entrance. You will be turned away if you go to the wrong gate. I suggest driving to the lot the day before to find the gate you will use.

When to Arrive at the Interview

You and the interviewer will agree upon a time for the interview.

Be on time. With all the maps and planning tools at your disposal, you do not have an excuse. Los Angeles traffic is notorious, so plan for delays.

If your interview is at a coffee shop, arrive 10-15 minutes early and enter the coffee shop 5 minutes early. You are probably not their only interviewee, so if you see them talking with another person, wait until they finish before walking over to introduce yourself.

If your interview is on a studio lot, arrive 20-25 minutes early. Lots are enormous, and you often have to park far away from the building you need to get to. You'll have to follow a map to the building, so give yourself time in case you get lost. If you find your building right away, wait outside until 5 minutes before your interview. You want to avoid stressing out the interviewer by arriving too far ahead of your scheduled time.

What to Bring

Bring a printed copy of your resume. If you think you'll meet multiple people, bring multiple copies of your resume.

Bring a good attitude. You would be amazed at the number of people who go to an interview and then complain about the job or the interview process. You're there to sell your skills to this potential employer. Sell with a smile, and save your complaints for your close friends.

Bring your personality. If you are interviewing, then the employer thinks you have the skills needed for the job. They're using this time to double-check that you weren't lying and are fun to be around. If you struggle with letting your personality shine through professionally, I highly recommend the book *Humor, Seriously* by Dr. Jennifer Aaker and Naomi Bagdonas.

You can find that book and a list of other resources at: https://www.tv-ae.com/resources.

What to Wear

Dress like you.

The film and television industry is casual and creative and is okay with casual and creative clothing. However, even in relaxed industries, you need to cover your body. For example, most people and places find crop tops to be unprofessional. Avoid clothing with stains, especially at the armpits. Get rid of shirts with wonky collars that have survived too many washes. Make sure you don't look rumpled. An iron can do a lot for everyone. Your outfits don't need to be bland, but they do need to be professional.

If dressing like you includes make-up, then wear make-up. On the other hand, if you feel more comfortable without make-up, then don't add it.

In every industry, you need hygiene. Take regular showers and get haircuts regularly. Brush your teeth. Wear deodorant. If you like perfume or body spray, use it sparingly because some people are sensitive to smell. You might feel like this is stating the obvious, and well, you'd be right. That said, an interviewer will draw conclusions based on how you present yourself regardless of what you find comfortable outside of work.

Create Your Elevator Pitch

Similar to your cover letter, have an elevator pitch about you ready to go. Your interviewer will probably say, "Tell me about yourself," and you will want to have an answer. Write it out and refine it. Get your answer down to a few solid sentences.

Here are some starting points:

1. Introduce yourself. What's your name? Where are you from originally?
2. What makes you unique? What's a fun hobby of yours?
3. What are your career goals? Do you want to be an editor eventually? Tell them!
4. Find a good way to hand the conversation back over to your interviewer. It's easy to have a great elevator pitch and then end with, "So... umm... yeah." Find a solid end sentence like, "That's why I applied for this job. It seems like it would be a good fit for me."

You don't need to answer every question above. However, remember to show a little personality. Let your passions shine through. And above all - let the interviewer know you're interested in the job! You would be amazed by how many people don't show interest in the position they're applying for, even if they want it.

Here is an example of an elevator pitch:

"My name is Jane Doe. I grew up in Miami, Florida and moved out to Los Angeles after I graduated from NYU's Tisch School of the Arts with a Bachelor's Degree in Cinema Studies. Outside of work, I'm obsessed with solar eclipses and I spent my gap-year before college traveling around the world to watch them. I applied for *Super Fake TV Show* because I have wanted to be an editor since I was 12 years old, and I'm looking for ways to be in the cutting room. This job seems like the perfect starting point for my career."

Here is another example of an elevator pitch:

"My name is Jane Doe. I moved out to Los Angeles about two months ago to start my career in post production. Eventually, I want to be a visual effects editor. I have been in love with blockbuster action films for as long as I can remember. I used to watch every behind-the-scenes feature I could find. I spent way too many hours with a bad green screen trying to recreate effects. I applied for this job because it seems like it will be an effects heavy film, and I think it would be a good learning opportunity for me."

Notice how Jane Doe tailored her elevator pitch to reflect the job. She added some fun personality moments but ultimately brought it back to the topic at hand - the interview.

If you struggle with memorizing things, or you think your elevator pitch will feel robotic when you recite it, then switch to bullet points instead. Write out some thoughts the day before so they're fresh in your head.

Here is an example of a bullet point approach:

- Jane Doe
- Miami to NYU to Los Angeles
- Eclipses
- Position = Post PA for *Super Fake TV Show*

Interviewing is a Skill

Remember that interviewing is a skill. It takes practice. You can get rusty. It takes time to be good at it.

If you've done everything above to prepare but still feel nervous about your upcoming interview, call a friend. Ask your friend to sit down with you and do a fake interview. Then, have them ask you questions and give you honest feedback on your answers.

Remember that your interviewer has asked you to interview for a reason. You passed the first round of applicants because they liked your resume and cover letter. You deserve to be there.

If it doesn't go well, take 5 minutes at home to write down what you can do better next time. After those 5 minutes, that interview is now in the past. You can move on and prepare for the next interview.

THE FIRST DAY

Congratulations! You got the job. The first day is a busy one. Let's talk about how to be prepared.

Things to Bring

Put your supervisor's phone number in your phone the day before you start. Then, you'll know who to call if you need help or are locked out of the office when you arrive.

You'll need to bring a few items to your first day. For a comprehensive list, check out our checklist on the following page.

POST PRODUCTION ASSISTANT
FIRST DAY CHECKLIST
FROM WWW.TV-AE.COM

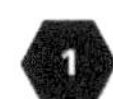 **THINGS TO BRING**

Identification for Your I9 (ie. Passport, Permanent Resident Card, etc)

Drivers License

Your Car's License Plate Number and VIN (Very Important on a Lot)

Checkbook (For a Voided Check for Direct Deposit)

Laptop, Charger, and Headphones

Notebook and Pen

 **FIRST DAY TO-DO**

Introduce Yourself to the Team and Learn All Names

Fill Out Start Paperwork

Obtain Badge and Keys Needed for Office Access

Learn About Your Daily and Weekly Tasks

Ask How Petty Cash Works

Ask About Your Weekly Crafty Budget

Learn How to Submit Receipts

Ask If You Can Set Up an Office Calendar

Ask Team if They Need Supplies Ordered

Learn Your Team's Food Allergies for Crafty and Lunch

Create a Take-Out Binder with Menus

Be Ready to Set Some Tasks Aside If Your Boss Has Other
Priorities

Identification

The most important thing is a form of identification that shows both your identity and employment authorization. In the USA, the easiest form of identification is your passport. If you don't have a passport, see the list in the Start Paperwork section. You'll need identification to get paid, so remember it!

Laptop

Some jobs require that you have a laptop, and others do not. Be sure to ask. They'll want you to have a laptop and not a tablet. You need to easily connect to the printer and you need to be able to type quickly.

Notebook

Your notebook is the strongest tool in your arsenal. Keep it with you at all times and use it to keep track of tasks. Check off work as you get it done so you know you have completed your work for the day. Be secure in the knowledge that you have not forgotten anything because it is all written down.

What to Wear

Read over the What to Wear to an Interview Section above and follow the same basic rules. Be yourself, but be professional. If the office is on a studio lot, you'll be required to get an ID badge. They'll take your photo for this badge, so be sure to be camera-ready on your first day.

Offices can be cold, so bring layers. You might want a sweatshirt or sweater: something you can remove when you venture out into the hot sun.

As a post PA, you'll be doing a lot of fetching and carrying, so wear shoes that will support you throughout the day. Stick to sneakers or flats.

Be Prompt

There is an old phrase that still resonates:
Early is on time, on-time is late, and late is unacceptable.

Traffic happens! Give yourself an extra 20 minutes in case you get caught up in a red-zone.

If your office is on a studio lot (especially the Universal or Warner Brothers lot), plan to arrive there with lots of time to spare. As a PA, they'll put your car in a far-away parking lot, and you'll need that extra time to get to the office. It can be a 15-minute walk, and it's easy to get lost when you're first learning. Extra time is crucial if this is your first time on that studio lot.

Be Friendly and Keep a Good Attitude

A good attitude is vital. It's hard to stay friendly when stressed, but it might mean the difference between a promotion and not being asked back next season. A good attitude is important in the feature film world too. Feature film post teams are tight-knit and often move from project to project as a crew. Your attitude could be the difference between being invited onto the next project or not.

Listen when introduced to people and work hard to remember their names. It's okay to ask again later for a refresher, but have everyone's name down by the end of day two.

Accept tasks with grace and not groans. One of the biggest reasons PAs are not asked back for a second season is because they were perceived to have a bad attitude. There will be jobs that are hard or seem menial. Do them anyway, and try your best to do them with a smile.

Start Paperwork

"Start Paperwork" is the umbrella term for the packet of paperwork that you need to read through, fill out, and sign when you begin your new job. This packet usually includes tax paperwork like a W-2 or 1099, employment and identity verification like an I-9, a direct deposit authorization form which will require a voided check, a deal memo which details how much you are being paid and the expected hours of a typical work week, a box rental, a vehicle information form, and a nondisclosure agreement. The start paperwork packet takes a long time to fill out so don't put it off until the very end of the day.

Tax Paperwork

For tax paperwork in the United States, you need to know your social security number. Be sure to have it memorized for your first day of work.

If you do not have a social security number, speak with your employer ahead of time so you know what you need to bring in for your paperwork.

Identification

Your employment verification will require that you have proof of identification. In the United States, this proof might include your passport, your driver's license and social security card, your military ID and birth certificate, or your perma-nent resident card (commonly called a Green Card). For a full list of appropriate identification, go to https://www.uscis.gov/i-9-central/form-i-9-acceptable-documents.

If you are unsure which document is appropriate, ask your direct supervisor, or ask your accounting department. Make sure you have the appropriate form of identification. They cannot pay you until you prove your identity.

Deal Memo

Your deal memo will have your hourly or weekly pay rate. It will also outline how and when overtime pay comes into effect. Only some films or television shows will allow over-time, so be sure to read your deal memo.

The deal memo will also state the length of a typical work week. In Los Angeles, a 60-hour work week is not uncommon. I hope that such long work weeks will be forced out of the culture, but a 12-hour day is relatively typical for now.

Box Rental

A Box Rental is compensation in exchange for use of per-sonal property. When you bring your laptop to work, you are technically leasing your personal property to your employer for use. When I was a post production assistant, I was given $5 per day for use of my laptop, which equaled a $25 per week box rental. This box rental usually has a cap. For instance, a $500 cap for the year.

Your box rental paperwork will have the details of your particular box rental. It will also ask you to fill in information like the brand and age of your laptop so they know the value of the item.

Vehicle Information Form

A Vehicle Information Form is usually only used on a studio lot or at a location where parking needs to be closely monitored. This form will ask for your vehicle make and model, the VIN number, and the license plate. They will put this information on file so you can easily access the company parking lots.

You may also be given a parking pass which needs to hang on your car's rear view mirror or placed in a side window.

Nondisclosure Agreements and Confidentiality

Some shows and movies will ask you to sign a nondisclosure agreement. According to Oxford Languages, a nondisclosure agreement is "a contract by which one or more parties agree not to disclose confidential information that they have shared with each other as a necessary part of doing business together." This contract is fairly standard in the film and television industry. The secret information is usually the script and significant plot points, but this contract could also cover information like the cast, the major department heads, or the shooting location. Be sure to read through the contract and make sure you understand it. You need to know the rules and what happens if you break the rules. Breaking the rules in this context could mean legal action against you.

> ***TIP:** Telling close friends or family about a project equals breaking your nondisclosure agreement, even if they're outside of the film and television industry. Your trust in your loved ones is not legally binding - the contract you signed is. Don't break the nondisclosure agreement.

A social media memo usually accompanies a nondisclosure agreement. This memo outlines what you can post to social media or other online sites. Some networks or producers encourage social media posting, but they might have strict rules about things that would be considered a spoiler. Be sure to read through this memo before posting any photos or talking about the plot online.

It's important to keep the inner workings of the show or movie to yourself even if you didn't sign a nondisclosure agreement. You don't want to be responsible for a major plot point leaking or for being the source that shares that a major star has left the project.

DAY TO DAY

Success is not defined by a single moment. Success is showing up every day and trying your hardest. Each day is an opportunity to build your future. Take this job seriously, and people will notice your dedication.

Definitions

There are many industry-specific terms out there. As you work, you will pick up these phrases quickly. However, there are four that are vital for a post production assistant. They are: cutting room, runs, dailies, and closed sets.

Cutting Room

A "cutting room" is simply another term for the post production office. It harkens back to the days when film was physically cut and reattached to create an edit. This is an umbrella term for the office as a whole. If you want to refer specifically to the room where the editor works, it is often referred to as an "edit bay" or simply a "bay."

Runs

A "run" is the general term for an errand outside of the office. A post PA's job can include a lot of runs like delivering things to and from various departments, picking up people, coffee or meals, or going grocery shopping.

Dailies

"Dailies" are the unedited footage that come from set and go to post production. They are delivered at the end of each shooting day. They are delivered digitally either by putting them onto an external harddrive or by sending them over a secure internet feed.

As a post production assistant, you will interact with dailies in two ways. 1) You may be tasked with picking up the harddrive from the dailies facility and delivering it to the post production office. 2) You may be tasked with creating a playlist on a dailies viewing system, like PIX, and sending that playlist to crew members for review. See the Dailies Review Systems section for more information on this task.

Closed Sets

A "closed set" is a filming location that is closed off from the majority of crew members in order to film sensitive scenes which might include nudity, intimacy, or a highly-secure plot point. It's rare for a post production assistant to encounter a closed set, but it's important to know about. If you are delivering something to a set and you notice that it is a closed set, be sure to ask if you're allowed to enter.

If you are charged with sending out dailies on a dailies viewing system each morning, do not send footage from a closed set without checking with your direct supervisor. Oftentimes, footage from a closed set can only go to certain crew members for review.

Ask for Work

One of the most significant pieces of advice that I wish I had listened to early in my career is to "ask for work." For a long time, I was under the impression that someone would tell me to work if there was work. I felt like I was a good worker because I accomplished what was given to me. However, that's not the thinking of a go-getter or a self-starter.

Start each day with a conversation with your direct supervisor. Bring your notebook! On a TV show, your immediate supervisor might be the post coordinator; on a feature, your supervisor might be the assistant editor. Ask them which tasks should be finished today. Write all your tasks down in your notebook so you can check them off as you accomplish the task.

Clarify the priorities. Try to prioritize the assignments your-self and then ask your supervisor if you got the order correct. Adjust as needed. If you have too much on your plate, then ask for help prioritizing tasks. For example, your supervisor might remove some items or push them later in the week in order to help your workload. Then get to work!

If you run out of work during the day, return to your super-visor and ask for more work. Always be looking to help out. Sometimes, there's nothing for you to do, but don't let that discourage you from asking every day. Remember that every task, big or small, contributes to the overall production and gives you interactions with people who are doing what you want to do and the opportunity to observe and learn. These opportunities can be active or passive experiences, but you will get the most out of them by being present and positive.

> ***TIP:** Keep your notebook and task lists professional and professional looking. You never know who might see it and what you've written or drawn. This isn't to say you can't doodle, but you don't want your boss seeing, "Call that person I hate" on your to-do list.

There are shows, especially first-season shows, where the post-team will only have enough time to do their assigned tasks. They will be exhausted. If you are proactive and take pride in your work, you take a burden off their shoulders. They never need to stress about finding time to make a cup of coffee. It will be available and hot when they need it because you took the time to do your job well. Meeting the team's needs is noticed, and people appreciate it even if they don't take the time to say thank you.

Remember Repetitive Tasks

There are things that you will need to do weekly or monthly. Have them clearly stated on your calendar so you remember, and then follow through with them. Every Monday might be grocery shopping day. You'll start the day by going to the grocery store to pick up snacks for the office. By having grocery day on your calendar, your boss won't have to ask every week for you to complete a task that should be automatic. Doing regular tasks without needing to be reminded shows that you're taking initiative in your work.

How to Handle a Mistake

We all make mistakes, and they are never fun. First, own up to your mistake and take responsibility. Then, let your boss know how you're working on fixing your error. Or, if it cannot be fixed, let your boss know that you have learned a lesson and it won't happen again. If your mistake has created a problem you don't know how to solve, ask for help. Your supervisors have more work experience than you do, and they might have encountered the situation before and will know how to fix it. They will also be able to help with any office politics that might need to be navigated.

Listen if someone pulls you aside to give you advice or to ask you to tweak a work habit. They are speaking with you because they believe in your career. They want you to succeed and are helping you to do so. Take their advice to heart and try your best to apply it.

Be kind if someone else makes a mistake. Remember that we're all human and we're all trying our best. Follow the edict "Praise in public, criticize in private." This sentiment stands true for email correspondence as well. If someone makes a mistake in an email, let them know in a side email so they can fix it for the group. Never reply-all to let someone know they have made an error.

Emails

Email is the main form of communication for a post production office. It's important to be polite and succinct in your emails. Ask your direct supervisor if you should be cc'ing them on all emails or only on specific emails. Some supervisors want to see all communications so they can easily stay up to date.

Include a show code in your subject line. The show code is the three or four-letter representation of the show's title. It is used in file names, emails, and communication shorthand. Ask your post supervisor or coordinator for the code at the beginning of the show. You are not in charge of inventing the show code, so be sure to ask!

Using your show code on every email you send for work is important. Post production assistants are usually only on one show at a time. However, you are responsible for communicating with many different departments. For example, corporate post production supervisors (common on features), dailies and online facilities, visual effects, sound teams, music supervisors, and more departments work on multiple shows simultaneously.

Example:

The name of the show is *This Fake Television Show.*

The show code could be "TFTS," or "FTS," or "TFS." When I asked my post supervisor, they told me the official code is TFS.

Remember, you are not in charge of inventing the show code.

> ***TIP:** If you're on a high-security show (like a Marvel show), ask if you're allowed to use the actual show code or if they have a fake code that you should use to protect communications.

Put Yourself In Their Shoes

Imagine yourself in one of the previously mentioned departments. If you're working on multiple shows, you need to prioritize. Of course, every show your department is working on is important, but sometimes a show with a deadline today at 5 pm must come before a show with a deadline next Friday. Therefore, you need a quick way to scan your email for updates from your priority show.

It Takes Two to Tango

Is someone else's inbox your concern? Sort of! If your email has a subject line that seems like spam, a personal communication, or a low priority, you will not get a reply in a timely manner, or worse, you won't get a reply at all. Making your email work-related helps to guarantee a response.

Use It All The Time

You might look at this and say, "Well, if only outside departments need the code, then why should I use it all the time?"

Let's be honest; if it's not a habit, you won't remember. But, on the other hand, if you use the code for every email, you don't need to stop and analyze who you're sending an email to. It can be automatic and, therefore, always remembered.

Compare These Subject Lines

Subject: That Spaceship Shot
Subject: TFS - VFX Fix Needed ASAP - Shot TFS_01_020

If you were on the visual effects team, which email would you answer first?

Email Signatures

It can be tempting to immediately update your email signature with your new job title. Make sure you check in with your direct supervisor before updating your signature. If you're on a high-profile show, you might need to keep the title of the show out of your signature.

Other items to have in your email signature:

· Your pronouns
· Your email address
· Your phone number

Items you do not need in your email signature:

· Quotes or song lyrics that are not work appropriate
· Your headshot

Dailies Review Systems

As previously stated, a post production assistant might be tasked with sending each day's dailies to certain crew members or stakeholders. There are a few different systems that are used for this process. The system is usually a desktop app or an online program. The most common systems are called PIX, Frame.iO, and DAX. You will be trained on the job for your particular system. However, these systems work in a fairly similar manner, and at its most basic level, you will create a playlist with selected footage and then send that playlist to a predetermined list of people.

The predetermined lists of people are called "distribution lists" or "distro lists." It is not a post production assistant's duty to update the distro lists. That's usually a job for the post supervisor or post coordinator. If you are tasked with updating or creating a distro list, then make sure that a supervisor looks over your lists and approves them before they go into use. The distro lists are highly political and often regulated by guild rules from guilds like the Directors Guild, the Screen Actors Guild, or the Producers Guild. So do not mess with the distro lists.

Regular Paperwork

The majority of a post production assistant's duties concerning paperwork are to email or print and distribute physical copies to the team. The exact paperwork that you are responsible for will vary from show to show. Talk with your direct supervisor so you know what you are responsible for.

Become good friends with your printer. A post-production assistant's job is to print paperwork and maintain the printer when it is jammed, out of ink, or lacking paper. Read up on your particular printer to make sure you can service it as needed.

A note on color printer ink: it is expensive, and you may not be cleared to purchase anything other than black ink. Check with your supervisor and try to print mostly in black and white. Below are some common types of paperwork you may encounter.

Calendar and At-A-Glance

The Calendar is a day-by-day overview of the deadlines for the show or film. Your supervisor will provide you with the completed calendar and you will print it out or email as instructed. The calendar is updated regularly, be sure to have the most up-to-date calendar at your desk so you are aware of deadlines.

The At-A-Glance is a single piece of paper with a chart that includes all major deadlines and their dates. This allows you to see deadlines "at-a-glance" without flipping through the calendar. The at-a-glance is updated with the calendar, be sure to have the most up-to-date version as well.

Call Sheets

The Call Sheet is a piece of production paperwork that lists a single day's shooting location, date, time, scenes to be shot, and required cast and crew. The call sheet is often printed and hung up in the post production offices to allow the team to access the information quickly. The call sheet is printed on legal-size paper.

Wifi Posters

The Wife Poster is a piece of paper hung up in each office that provides the wifi name and password. Hang these up on your first day so no one has to search for the wifi password.

> ***TIP:** Some high-security shows do not allow the wifi to be posted. Ask your direct supervisor before creating and hanging wifi posters.

Phone Sheets

In an office where the team has landline office phones, you will need to create a small piece of paper to tape near each phone which contains a list of common phone extensions for easy reference. For example, this list might include "Post Supervisor - John Doe - Ex. 332." Talk with your direct supervisor to see if they prefer a specific format for the phone sheets. Hierarchy and job titles matter on these sheets, so be sure to have the list approved before you place them in each office.

Use the Phone

I hated answering the phone and making calls as a PA. However, it's an essential part of the job. Talk with your direct supervisor to see if there's a way they would prefer you answer the phone. For example, to help with privacy, your boss may instruct you to answer the phone with "Editorial" rather than "Post Production Offices for This Fake Television Show, this is Jane."

Always smile while on the phone. Even a fake smile helps your body to remember to keep a note of friendliness in your voice as you talk. There's an audible difference in tone, and a friendly tone can help keep conversations on track.

Practice transferring a phone call. As the post production assistant, you will be the first point of contact in the office. Executives, directors, or other departments will call in and ask for various people within your department. Make sure you know how to transfer the phone call without hanging up on the caller. If you have never had to transfer a phone call before and are unsure how that process works, be sure to ask. If this is the first time anyone in the office has used this phone system, it's your job to find the manual and figure out the system. The model number for the phone is often on the back or bottom of the phone. You can do an online search for the model number with the word "manual," and you can usually find the instructions for the phone.

When I was first acquainting myself with making phone calls, I often hung up the phone only to realize that I didn't get all the information I needed. So I found a system to help me communicate clearly. Before making a call, write the talking points on a sticky note. Bullet them so they're nice and clear, and check in with your bullet points throughout the call.

For example:

Call Restaurant for Team Lunch

- Make a reservation for eight people on Monday at 1 pm
- Ask if they can accommodate a nut allergy
- Tell them about Lisa's birthday and ask about a small dessert.

When you have discussed every bullet point, double-check your list to ensure you have all the information you need before you hang up the phone.

Voicemail

When leaving a voicemail, be sure to give your name, your callback number, and your reason for calling. Most people will only return a call with a voicemail. They assume that if it's important, you will leave a message.

Here's a voicemail format that I have found works well for me:

> "Hi, my name is _______ with the show _______. I'm calling about _______. Please give me a callback. My phone number is _______. Again, that number is _______, and this is __[name]__."

Most people forget to take notes when listening to a voicemail. By book-ending the phone call with your name, you're giving them time to grab a notebook or a sticky note so they can write down your information. You'll notice that I suggest repeating the phone number. It's easy to miss a digit while listening to a voicemail, so saying the number twice helps people get it down right.

Driving

Driving to pick up people or things is a big part of a post production assistant's job. Keep your car clean and the seats accessible. You never know what will be asked of you, and you won't want to scramble to clean out your car.

Los Angeles is notorious for confusing parking information. Be sure to check the street signs when you park to make sure you're parked legally. You don't want to spend your hard-earned money on parking tickets. Your job will not reimburse you for parking tickets.

Your job will reimburse you for parking fees from a parking structure or lot. Grab a receipt and add it to your petty cash filing system if you need to pay for a parking garage. See the Receipts and Petty Cash section for more information.

Your job is not worth your life. Obey traffic signs, speed limits, and construction warnings. Do not text and drive. Wear your seatbelt. The deadline you're trying to hit is not worth compromising your safety.

Mileage

Post production assistants are reimbursed for mileage when traveling for work. As of January 1st, 2023, the California reimbursement rate is 65.5 cents per business mile. The reimbursement rate varies state to state, so be sure to look it up. Keep track of where you drive, and keep track of your odometer. Accounting will often ask for an odometer reading as part of the required paperwork for mileage reimbursement. Check your pay stubs to make sure you were reimbursed.

Golf Carts

On large studio lots, you might be issued a golf cart for use by your team. As a post production assistant, it's your job to ensure that the golf cart is charged or gassed up, clean, and easily available for the team. You also keep track of the key.

Electric golf carts need to be charged when they're not in use. The golf cart charger will often be on the side of your office building. Make sure the cart is plugged in each night before you leave. Gas-powered golf carts need to be filled with gas, just like a car. Talk with your supervisor about how you get gas. For instance, the NBC Universal Lot has its own gas station on the studio lot where you can charge the gas directly to your show by telling them the show's name and your post supervisor's name.

In a bustling office, it might be easy to lose the golf cart key. Talk with your supervisor about implementing a check-out system for the golf cart. If the key is missing, you can quickly identify who used the cart last. More often than not, they forgot to return it and the key is in their pocket.

Be sure to clean off the golf cart after it rains or if it is particularly dusty outside. Los Angeles gets wildfires and lots of pollen, and the particles can build up on vehicles. No one wants to sit in water or dirt, so keep it tidy for your team.

Obviously, the golf cart is not a toy and should not be taken out for joyrides or used recklessly.

Office Supplies

As a post production assistant, you are essentially the manager of the local general store. You're responsible for ensuring that office supplies like binders, highlighters, pens, printer ink, and more, are available. Your team will stop by and assume that you can supply them with everything they need.

Most studios have a storage facility where they keep semi-permanent office supplies like hole punches, staples, and tape dispensers. Talk with your direct supervisor to see if this storage space is an option for your team. Shop the storage space first, then purchase whatever else the office needs.

***TIP:** Any time you spend money, be sure to run it by someone higher up than you.

Here is a list of office supplies that should be available for the post team:

- Two binders for each episode. One binder is for the editor, and the second is for the assistant editor. They'll use these binders to store the paperwork received from the set. A 2 or 3-inch 3-ring binder is usually preferred.
- Pens
- Mechanical pencils with good erasers
- Highlighters in multiple colors
- Post-It Notes - 2 inch
- Post-It Note flags
- A three-hole punch
- A two-hole punch for the call sheets
- Legal-sized clipboards for each office. These are used to display the call sheets for each day.
- Stapler
- Staples
- Tape dispenser
- Tape
- Brads. These are metal tabs used to hold scripts together without a binder.

After you stock up on office supplies, check the supplies regularly to keep them from being depleted. Purchase new items as needed.

Coffee

I think the film industry would fall to pieces without coffee. There are hard days when a hot cup of coffee is the only thing that keeps you going, and it's incredibly important that you know how to make coffee. I know that many of you already know how to make coffee. If you feel like this section does not apply to you, please read the ***TIPS**. Otherwise, feel free to skim through this section.

Basic Drip Coffee Maker

A drip coffee maker is the most common version you will encounter. Please see the diagram below.

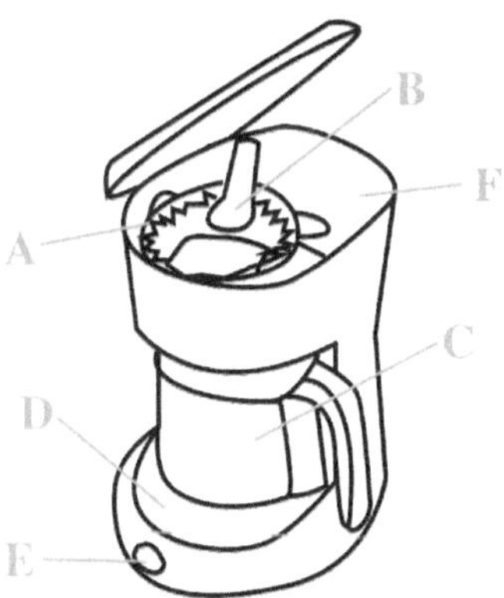

Each machine will vary slightly. Be sure to read the manual for the specific machine you are using. In general, to make coffee in a drip coffee maker, you need to:

1. Make sure the machine is turned off but plugged in.
2. Open the top of the top of the machine and check to see if used coffee grounds are in the basket (A). If there are used coffee grounds, move the water spout (B) by sliding or rotating it to the side. Lift out the plastic basket (A) with the filter and the old coffee grounds. Holding onto the basket, empty the basket into a trashcan to dispose of the filter and the used coffee grounds. Do not throw away the plastic basket.
3. Return the plastic basket (A) to its place in the machine.
4. Remove the coffee pot (C) (also called a carafe) from the warming plate (D). The coffee pot may be hot, so hold the pot by the handle and use caution. The warming plate also gets hot. Do not touch the warming plate.
5. Empty the coffee pot of any remaining old coffee.
6. Clean and rinse out the coffee pot.
7. Fill the coffee pot with water up to the appropriate level for the amount of coffee you are making. For example, fill with water to the "4" line for four cups of coffee. Some post teams prefer that you use filtered water for this step instead of water from the tap.
8. Pour the coffee pot's water into the machine's back water basin (F).
9. Place the coffee pot back on the warming plate.
10. Put a new filter into the plastic basket.
11. Scoop ground coffee into the filter-lined basket. The general rule of thumb is one to two tablespoons of coffee per six ounces of water, but exact measurements will be up to your personal preferences. For example, we want 4-8 tablespoons of coffee grounds to make our 4 cups of coffee. Most Americans prefer stronger coffee.

12. Return the water spout (B) to its regular position over the basket.
13. Close the top of the machine.
14. Turn on the machine (E). Most machines will auto-brew when you turn it on, however, double-check the manual for your model to ensure you do not need to press additional buttons.
15. Wait patiently for the coffee to brew. Be sure to watch the first few drips before attending to other tasks. This way, you know that the coffee is brewing correctly.

Troubleshooting: If the coffee machine is not working, double check that it's plugged in. If it's plugged in, try moving it to a different outlet.

***TIP:** Most drip coffee machines have an auto-brew feature. Set up the machine with fresh grounds and water each night so it auto-brews the next morning 10 minutes before the team usually arrives at the office. For example, if your team gets in at 9:00 am, set the auto-brew for 8:50 am. This preparation not only takes a task off your list in the morning but also provides the team with fresh coffee, even if you're out on a run that prevents you from being in the office first thing.

Pod Coffee Machines

Pod coffee machines have become increasingly common in post production offices. A brand-name version of this would be Keurig or Nespresso. You may have both a drip coffee machine and a pod espresso machine in your office kitchen. Pod machines have a water basin like a drip machine, but the coffee comes in a pre-measured, disposable container.

Be sure to check out the manual for your particular pod machine. There is a specific order for putting in the water vs. the pod, and it changes machine to machine. In general, throw away or recycle the pods after they're used, keep the machine clean, and keep the water basin filled.

Coffee Orders For Large Groups

Even if you don't drink coffee, you must know how to order it. There are a lot of strange coffee orders out there. You don't need to know what a "dirty chai latte with an extra pump" is, but you need to be able to say the name correctly over the phone. If someone asks for a type of coffee that you've never heard of before, ask them to repeat the name of it and even ask how to spell it if the words are unclear to you. If you don't understand what you're ordering, there's a big chance it will get muddled in translation to the barista. So take the time to get it down correctly.

***TIP:** Most coffee shops prefer large orders to be called in ahead of time or entered on their phone app. Calling ahead allows the shop to prioritize their one-coffee customers at the counter and lets them set aside large orders in their pick-up area.

Crafty

"Crafty" is the film industry term for snacks. It's a shortened version of the phrase "craft services." Crafty is different from paid meals or catered lunches because it is always available as a grab-and-go option. In contrast, catering or paid meals happen at a specific (often mandated) time, like a 1 pm lunch.

As a Post PA, you are in charge of crafty and the communal kitchen area. You're in charge of keeping snacks and drinks stocked and the sinks and countertops clean. Finally, and most importantly, you're responsible for keeping the coffee fresh and hot.

Keep a request list in the kitchen. A list lets team members ask for snacks they like and gives you a good baseline for shopping. After your weekly grocery shop, stock the refrigerator and the cupboards in a tidy manner. If you have a large box of individually wrapped snacks, take the time to unload them from the giant snack box so the packets are easy to grab in a hurry.

Throughout the day, check the kitchen area to ensure it's clean. I personally do not think it's a PA's job to wash dishes.

Working adults can wash their own coffee mugs. However, most places will expect you to clean up dishes as part of your job. People leave dirty dishes in communal kitchens, and you will need to wash those dishes. Dirty or messy kitchens are not inviting, and they add a layer of stress to a busy office. Help your team stay happy by keeping the kitchen area free of dirty dishes, trash, and half-eaten food items. Clean out the refrigerator every Friday, but have a system so people can save their leftovers.

If dishes stack up regularly in the kitchen and begin to be your only task, talk with your direct supervisor about putting up a fun sign to remind people to wash their dishes. Remember to always be polite, even in quick written-word communications.

Meals

One of the primary duties of the post production assistant is to get meals for the team. It's easy to feel like this is an unimportant task. However, according to a study by the Departments of Neurosurgery and Physiological Science of the University of California at Los Angeles School of Medicine, eating promotes synaptic activity and contributes to learning and memory (Gómez-Pinilla, 21). In essence, work is easier when you're well-fed. Your ability to deliver a meal on time contributes to a successful workday. You are one of the keys to productivity.

Ask your direct supervisor if the show is paying for any meals. Some shows pay for lunch but not dinner, and they will always have a limit on the cost of a meal. Also, ask the amount that you're allowed to tip. For example, most studios only enable you to tip 5% on a takeaway meal.

Legally, meal breaks are required every 6 hours. Most post production teams eat lunch at 1:00 pm, which puts dinner at 7:30 pm. Most productions will end the day before official dinner time. However, some shows might require the post team to work late. Ask your direct supervisor beforehand if you are required to pick up dinners and if the show pays for dinners. If picking up dinner will put you into overtime pay, make sure you clear staying late with your supervisor.

Notes on Meals: You are not there to comment on what people eat. You are not their doctor; therefore, you have no reason to comment on what they eat or how much or how little they eat. You are there to take their order and get food to them on time. Allergies are always serious. Always note down an allergy and make sure it is communicated to the restaurant.

Example Timeline

Lunch at 1:00 pm means people must have food in hand at 1:00 pm. So, you need to back-time the order process to get meals to everyone on time. Below is a suggested timeline. Of course, you need to adjust this depending on the restaurant's proximity to your office.

- 4:30 pm - Call the restaurant you plan to order from tomorrow and ensure they will be open. Ask how they want large orders submitted. Some places have a particular fax number or email address for large orders.
- End of the Work Day - Send an email with tomorrow's lunch location, a link to the menu, and a deadline for submitting an order.

> ***TIP:** BCC everyone on the email, so if someone accidentally hits reply-all, it will return just to you and won't flood everyone's inboxes.

- The Next Morning - Copy and paste each person's order into an easy-to-view order form. Please see the following page for an example.
- 10:00 am - Send a reminder email that the order deadline is approaching.
- 10:30 am - Finalize all orders and finish adding them to the order form.

- 10:45 am - Submit your order to the restaurant by calling, faxing, emailing, or submitting an online order form. If you fax, email, or submit an online order form, always call the restaurant 5 minutes later to ensure they received your order.
- 12:15 pm - Leave to pick up the meals. Bring your order form and a pen.
- 12:30-12:45 pm - Pick up the order from the restaurant. Check every single meal to make sure it's correct. Check them off on your order form so you know you have everything. If someone has an allergy, confirm that the restaurant took precautions. You can also take this time to put everyone's name on their food containers.
- 12:55 pm - Set out lunch in the common area. Make sure everyone has utensils and that their meal can be found easily.
- 1:00 pm - Alert everyone that lunch is available. Encourage people to take a break from their computers and sit together.

Meal Order Form Example

Restaurant Name: _______________________

Date: _____________

Picked Up?	Person	Order
	Cindy	Veggie burger with American cheese, side salad
	James	Quinoa bowl with harvest vegetables and feta cheese
	Pat	Chicken sandwich, side fries, gluten free bread. NOTE: GLUTEN ALLERGY
	Siobhan	Mac and Cheese Bowl

Receipts and Petty Cash

Keep track of your receipts and petty cash.

Petty cash is the money a show gives to a department for minor expenses. As a post production assistant, you will utilize petty cash to purchase office supplies, crafty, and daily meals. All petty cash must be accounted for, and missing petty cash can be a basis for firing you. This applies to every size bill and coin.

Some shows work on a reimbursement system. In those cases, you'll pay for something up-front, and the show will re-pay you with your next paycheck. I'm not too fond of this. A company should not borrow money from its lowest-paid employees. However, it happens. If you're on this type of show, it's important to note that the company won't reimburse you if you don't have a receipt, which means paying out of pocket for the show's expenses.

When you pay for anything for the show, with petty cash or as a reimbursement, ask the cashier for an itemized receipt. This receipt shows the cost of each item purchased. You are only reimbursed for a receipt with itemization because the company can prove the purchase was relevant to the show.

***TIP:** When you get a receipt, take a picture of it with your phone as a backup.

When you return to the office, immediately put the receipt into your organization system. Tape your receipts onto a receipt form and fill out the appropriate information. Please see the following page for a sample receipt form. Some studios have a specific form that they require you to use, and others will let you use your own template. Studios require that you send in the original receipts on a regular basis. You can store these receipt forms with attached receipts in a binder or in the envelope you will use to deliver the receipts to the accounting department or your department head.

> ***TIP:** Make a photocopy of the receipt form with the attached receipt and keep this backup in a binder in case the original is lost.

Keep track of your petty cash and ensure you're not running low. It's essential to have enough money to buy lunch.

Tape
Receipt
Here

Date: _______________

Store Name:

____

____

Total: _______________

Timecard

I had never seen a timecard until my first post production assistant job, and I needed help understanding how to fill it out. So, if you're like me, here's a breakdown. Please see the diagram on the next page.

PAYROLL COMPANY — CREW TIME CARD

SHOW					PROD#			GUAR HOURS	RATE		WEEK ENDING
This Fake Television Show											
NAME					SOCIAL SECURITY #			JOB CLASSIFICATION/OCC CODE			ACCOUNT#
Jane Doe					000-00-0000						
LOAN OUT					FEDERAL ID #			LOCATION			NY

WORK STATE	CITY	ACCT CODE	DATE	LOC	DAY	CALL	MEAL 1 OUT	MEAL 1 IN	MEAL 2 OUT	MEAL 2 IN	WRAP	RE RATE	OCC CODE	TOTAL HRS	1X	1.5X	2X	MEAL PNLTY	ACCT	RATE	TYPE	HRS	TOTAL
CA	Los Angeles				SUN																1X		
CA	Los Angeles				MON	8	13	13:30			19:30										1.5X		
CA	Los Angeles				TUE	8	13	13:30			19:30										2X		
CA	Los Angeles				WED	8	13	13:30			19:30										3X		
CA	Los Angeles				THU	8	13	13:30	19:30	20:00	22:00										4X		
CA	Los Angeles				FRI	8	13	13:30			19:30												
CA	Los Angeles				SAT																		

Layoff/Termination Date: / /

FOR ACCT'G PURPOSES ONLY

TOTAL HOURS

TOTAL AMOUNT

COMMENTS: Plus Mileage

ACCT#	MEALS ALLOW #61	MEALS TAX #61	PER DIEM ADV #56	ACCT#	CDN INCLASS OW #60	CDN INCL TAX #61	PER DIEM ADV #56	ACCT#	MEAL MONEY TAX #57
ACCT#	BOX RENTAL #53	ACCT#	CAR ALLOWANCE	ACCT#	MILEAGE ALLOW #52	MILEAGE TAX #58	MILEAGE ADV #56	ACCT#	2ND CAMERA #60
***CANADIAN SHOWS** - PLEASE SUPPLY ALLOWABLE TAXABLE CN PER DIEM IN U.S. $ AND CONV. RATE			AND	PER DIEM BASED ON: ______ DAYS @ ______ U.S $ PER DAY		CN PER DIEM ALLOW	CN PER DIEM TAX	ACCT#	SALARY ADVANCE #21
ACCT#	HAZARD #13	ACCT#		ACCT#		ACCT#		ACCT#	

PRODUCER AND EMPLOYEE ACKNOWLEDGE BY SIGNING THIS CARD THAT IF NO HOURS ARE RECORDED, EP WILL PRESUME THAT ONLY THE GUARANTEED HOURS WERE WORKED

EMPLOYEE SIGNATURE **X** _Jane Doe_   APPROVED **X** __________

On each timecard, you need to fill out the following:

- Show - Put the name of the show you're working on.
- Week Ending - This is the Saturday at the end of the week. If Friday this week is 4/21, your Week Ending date is 4/22.
- Name - Your full legal name. If you have a screen name or nickname, do not put that here.
- Social Security Number - After week one, you can usually put just the last four digits, but check with your accounting department to ensure that's okay.
- Work State - in this example, the work state is California (CA).
- Work City - in this example, the work city is Los Angeles.
- Date - Fill in the date column, starting with Sunday and ending with Saturday.
- Call Time - this is when you start in the morning. Don't lie about your times. Write them down accurately. If you ever need to file a workers' compensation claim, you must prove that you were at work when the accident happened. You can verify this by keeping accurate time records on your timecard.
- Meal 1 Out Time - The "Out Time" is when you begin lunch. You are out of the office. In this example, I use 24-hour time where 13 equals 1 pm. In my opinion, 24-hour time makes the math more straightforward, but that's a personal preference and not required.
- Meal 1 In Time - The "In Time" is when you finish lunch. You are in the office. Lunch, in this example, lasts for half an hour.

- You'll see in this example that Meal 2 is generally skipped, except for Thursday when this person worked overtime and needed to take a dinner break.
- Wrap - End of the work day. Make sure you end your day before you hit dinner, or make sure that you take a dinner break. You'll see that wrap is usually at 19:30 (7:30 pm), six hours after lunch ends at 13:30 (1:30 pm).
- Comments - This is where you can put other information. For this example, this person is letting accounting know they also submitted a mileage form.
- Employee Signature - sign your timecard.

Ask your direct supervisor where you should submit your timecard. They often need to be approved by the post producer or post supervisor before they are sent on to the accounting department.

What to Do When You're Stuck

Troubleshooting is a necessary skill in any career. However, I've seen that people who are new in their careers often forget to troubleshoot before asking for help. Before you ask for help, try to solve the problem independently. Online search engines, such as Google, are your best friend. You can solve most issues with a quick search. Always try to solve a problem independently unless the task is highly time-sensitive.

If you can't solve the problem alone then ask laterally before asking up the command chain. Talk to someone on the same hierarchical level as you. For example, if you're a post production assistant, you want to ask another support staff member. Some people on the support level may include: the writers' assistant, the director's assistant, or another post production assistant who has been at the company or on the show longer than you. If your lateral friends cannot help, then ask up one level. As a Post PA, this is usually the post coordinator or the assistant editor.

Asking for help is also a necessary skill. There will be times when you simply do not have enough knowledge to complete a task. That's ok. You are still an essential and valued team member if you ask questions. The critical thing to remember is to only ask a question once. Write it down or memorize it as soon as you understand the answer so you do not need to ask again later. You'll notice I said, "As soon as you under-stand the answer." You can ask for clarification if the answer doesn't make sense. You can request to have something ex-plained differently. Make sure you understand the answer to your question. Doing a task incorrectly can often cost more time down the road than asking for clarification now.

| 83 |

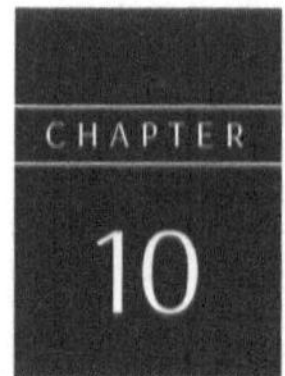

IN THE ROOM

One of the best ways to learn the dynamics of a cutting room is to sit in with the editor. Please ask for this opportunity. A post production assistant's job in the edit bay is to sit and listen. Sometimes, you will be expected to take notes. Most editors are happy to let you sit with them while they work on dailies or address easy notes. Editors even let PAs sit in and take notes for them during sessions with the producers or director. It is a privilege to be in the room, not a right. Treat it as such.

Listening

Sitting quietly and listening can be hard. This is especially true if you have an idea on how to fix a problem. It is the editor's job to fix the problem, suggest solutions, and field questions. You are there to observe. You are not there to entertain the director or producer. So, do not chit chat.

Your observation should be active and not passive. Pay attention to how the editor fields questions and navigates politics. Watch how the editor auditions cuts for themselves before showing them off to the producer or director in the room. Train your instincts. See if you can guess what the editor will do to address a note. Do you disagree with a note that the director or producer is giving? Ask yourself why. Dig in and find a satisfying reason.

Answering Questions

Some producers and directors are mentors at heart and will try to bring you into the process. This is a gift. When you get asked for an opinion - give an opinion. This shows that you have been actively listening and engaged in the work. Just remember, your opinion should never disparage anyone's work. Be diplomatic in your answer, but don't suck up to the big boss. If there's a problem with the story, then everyone in the room wants to fix it. They'll think less of you if you pretend nothing is wrong.

Sometimes, people in the editorial room can get passionate and intense. Tensions can run high. In a bad moment, someone in the room might try to use you as a tie-breaker. They'll ask for your opinion hoping you'll be on their side so they can win an argument. Of course, this is unfair to you, but it happens, and you need to know how to address it. Here are a few options:

· Ask a question in return. "You would like Character A to cross the room faster. Is that to remove the line said by Character B?" This might help clarify the intention of the note, or it might allow for a new line of discussion that hasn't been considered yet.

· Restate the two solutions on the table. "So, Editor is saying X, and you're saying Y. Do I have that right?" More often than not, they'll try to back up their statement and move on from you.

· If they really press you, default to the editor's opinion. This isn't to suck up to the editor. The editor has watched all of the dailies and has a general sense of what can and cannot work in the cut. If the editor is pushing back on a note, they might not have the necessary pieces to execute it effectively.

Note-Taking

Before a note-taking session, ask the editor if there is a specific way they like their notes formatted. Follow their directions. In these note sessions, a director or producer will usually be in the room. The director and producer get the seats in the room with the clear view of the TV or monitor, usually on the couch. Bring your own chair.

Take notes on your laptop and type quietly. Write down everything. The notes do not need to be straight dictation, but make sure you have each note written down. For example, if the Executive Producer says, "I'm not loving the way scene 5 goes into scene 6. Maybe it's a problem with the sound. Can we add a plane taking off and utilize that for the transition? It might help sell the movement in the next frame." You may write down, "Try a plane take-off sound for the scene 5 to scene 6 transition." Note down the timecode as often as you can. The timecode is displayed on the editor's client monitor in the top right or left. Always format your timecode the way it's formatted on the screen. Remember to listen and not to offer commentary unless asked.

> ***TIP:** Usually, the timecode format is hh:mm:ss:ff (h = hour, m = minute, s = second, f = frame). Most shows will begin at hour one (1) and not hour zero (0).

Think critically about the note-taking process and see if you can improve upon it. Once, I realized while taking notes for an editor that the editor addressed some notes with the director in the room and others later when the director was not there. So instead of deleting the notes the editor had addressed from my document, I crossed them out with a single strikethrough. That way, the editor could easily see the note was accomplished, and they have a reference for the notes in case they want to double-check them.

At the end of the notes session, ask the editor if they want the notes printed or emailed.

GRIT

"I can't control the amount of talent I have, but I can control how hard I work." - Christopher Rouse, ACE, during a 2014 talk at the American Cinema Editors Internship Series Lectures.

Angela Duckworth, the author of *Grit: The Power of Passion and Perseverance*, defines grit like this:

> "Grit is passion and perseverance for long-term goals.
>
> One way to think about grit is to consider what grit isn't.
>
> Grit isn't talent. Grit isn't luck. Grit isn't how intensely, for the moment, you want something.
>
> Instead, grit is about having what some researchers call an"ultimate concern"–a goal you care about so much that it organizes and gives meaning to almost everything you do. And grit is holding steadfast to that goal. Even when you fall down. Even when you screw up. Even when progress toward that goal is halting or slow.
>
> Talent and luck matter to success. But talent and luck are no guarantee of grit. And in the very long run, I think grit may matter as least as much, if not more." (Duckworth)

Grit is the number one ingredient to success in the film industry. Successful people are there because they stuck with it, worked hard, and kept their eye on the long-term prize. Moving up in the film and television hierarchy takes a long time, and it's hard to be patient. You hear stories of a break-out wunderkind all the time, but you don't see the decade of hard work that brought them to that break-out moment. You also don't hear about the people behind the scenes who have determinedly honed their craft to become the go-to person in their field. You do not need to be an industry rockstar to be successful. You simply need to keep going.

Goal-Setting

Here are a few tips for identifying and achieving your long-term goals.

First, visualize your future. Write out where you want to be in one year, five years, ten years, and at retirement. Focus on goals that you have control over. For example, winning an Oscar or Emmy Award would be amazing, but you do not have control over that outcome. Instead, focus on creating a network of intelligent, creative people you respect. Focus on working in the genre of film or television that you find creatively satisfying. Write out quantifiable goals. For example:

- In one year, I want to have five fantastic people that I can call as a reference.
- In five years, I want to be an assistant editor on a premium drama series.
- In ten years, I want to be an editor on a drama series.
- At retirement, I want to look back at my career and be thankful for all the great people I got to work with and all the creatively challenging shows I got to edit.

Next, look at these goals and translate them into short-term action items. For example, those bullet points require knowing people you like and respect, which means growing your network. Those goals also include being a skilled editor, which means practice, practice, practice. So, this year, concentrate on increasing your network, working hard at your day job so you know your references will vouch for you, and taking on one small editing project a month to add to your portfolio and grow your skills.

Finally, check in on your goals every quarter to ensure you're working toward them. The year's quarters are: Q1: January 1st – March 31st, Q2: April 1st – June 30th, Q3: July 1st – September 30th, Q4: October 1st – December 31st.

When I'm working on a long-term goal, I like to send a scheduled email to myself. This email will send itself to me at a later date, allowing "past me" to check on "present me." Draft an email addressed to yourself with the subject line, "Long-Term Goal Check-In," and in the body of the email write out a few questions and instructions for yourself. These questions can be whatever you want, but a few I like are:

- How's it going?
- Are you stuck anywhere? If so, how can you fix it?
- Can you ask for help from a friend?
- What's the next step?
- Put a date on your calendar for the next step.

When you finish your email draft, find the "scheduled send" menu instead of hitting send. In Gmail, scheduled send is in the arrow directly to the right of the send button, but it may reside elsewhere in your particular email program. Schedule the email to send one quarter from now. For example, if it's May 15th, schedule the email to send at 8:00 am on August 15th. On August 15th, this check-in email will arrive in your inbox. Do your self-check-in and then schedule the email to pop back up in the next quarter (November 15th).

If you find yourself blocked from your goals, take a good hard look at your steps. Ask yourself a few questions:

- Do I still want this goal?
- Am I actually at step one?
- Is there something I need to do before my current step one?
- What concrete things can I do <u>today</u> to help reach my goal?

Enjoy the Magic

Even with all these tools, the honest truth is, there will be difficult jobs and days when you feel like giving up on this crazy career. Find moments in your day to think about how great it is that you get to help create stories for a living. I remember being a Post PA on a feature film, and I got the opportunity to go to a scoring session. A scoring session is where a live band plays and records the musical score for the film. I stood behind the glass and watched as incredibly talented musicians put music to the scenes the editorial team had worked on for months. It took my breath away. I was so grateful to be in that room. Find moments to be thankful.

Find the things in the job that you enjoy. There's always something. My worst job came with the best view from my office. The upper-story window looked out over a plush golf course, and I saw a rainbow on more than one occasion. It brought me a sense of peace on a job with very little peace. That view was enough to get me through that one tough job.

Above all, keep going. There will be long days, and there will be magical days. Hold onto the magic.

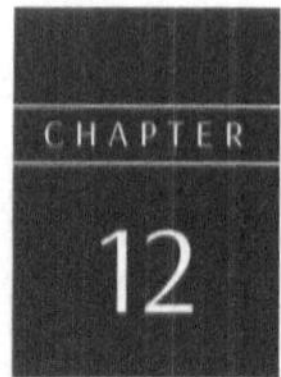

WHEN TO MOVE ON

The sentiment "keep going, no matter what," is great for long-term goal completion, however, it can accidentally keep you in a toxic work environment. There are jobs and relationships that are unhealthy. You do not need to stay in an unhealthy work environment.

Difficult Bosses vs. Toxic Bosses

A toxic boss is someone in a leadership role who causes damage to those they're entrusted to lead. This damage can be emotional or physical, and both are unacceptable.

Tough bosses, on the other hand, push you to make fewer mistakes, take on more responsibility, and improve your work. Someone can push you without being toxic. I would encourage sticking with a boss who pushes you to go the extra mile. You'll learn a lot from them.

Toxic bosses are different. An unhealthy workplace with a toxic boss could look like this:

- You are blamed for other people's mistakes.
- Your needs or requests are ignored or mocked.
- Name-calling, ostracizing, or pitting you against co-workers for your bosses time.
- Sexual harassment or misconduct.
- You are talked down to, dismissed, or mocked in relation to a protected category such as age, race, ethnicity, religion, gender, gender expression, or sexual orientation.
- You are humiliated as a punishment for a mistake.
- Intense micromanagement
- Your boss only offers criticism instead of constructive feedback.
- Your boss uses fear as a motivator.
- Your boss has intense anger reactions such as yelling, punching walls, or throwing objects.

If you find yourself in this type of environment, talk to an expert and then, if necessary, find a way to leave.

Talk to an Expert

Before leaving an unhealthy work environment, your first stop is to talk with Human Resources, also called HR. You can find the information for the Human Resources Department in your contact list. Sometimes bad behavior can be corrected. Take the time to go over your issues with HR and speak frankly about your experience. They have tools that can help someone examine their behavior and course-correct.

You can also talk with a professional, licensed, therapist. If you are feeling stuck or unhappy at work, you might benefit from the unbiased opinion of a therapist. Seek one out and chat with them about your concerns and how to address those concerns. Therapists can also help determine if your relationship with your boss or coworkers is healthy. If you are having thoughts of suicide or self-harm, please call the Suicide and Crisis Lifeline. In the United States, that number is 988.

Un-nurturing Workplaces

It can be easy to mistake an un-nurturing workplace for a toxic workplace. There are jobs that do not encourage you to grow. There are also points in your career where such a workplace could be very comfortable. We don't want to grow all the time. However, such workplaces can feel stifling if you're actively trying to advance. This is not a toxic workplace, it's just not the right place for you right now. A bad fit can be draining. If you have the ability to finish out the show or the season, then try to do so. If you know you're in the wrong place and you want to move on, then leave gracefully.

Leaving

Remember, this job opportunity is not your only opportunity. Sometimes the answer is to leave.

Create an exit plan. An exit plan will help you leave well. Write out the steps you need to complete so you can leave your current position. They might include: apply for new work, get hired on a new job, have two months of expenses in my savings account, or submit my notice to HR. Be sure to save your money in case you don't find work immediately or your next job falls through. Give two weeks' notice before you leave. How you leave a job can influence future hiring, so be sure to leave respectfully.

Early in my career, I was desperate to move out of working nights and into a day-time assistant editor position. As a result, I left a job with almost no notice. My post coordinator at the time called me out on it. He was right to do so, and I'm grateful for the feedback he gave me. Leaving a team without notice puts a significant burden on the group as they try to compensate for the absence of a team member, and it does not reflect well on you. Leave a job well. Give them time to find a replacement. Thank your coworkers for the things they have taught you.

Stay in touch with the coworkers you enjoy. The film and television industry is small, and you may get to work together again.

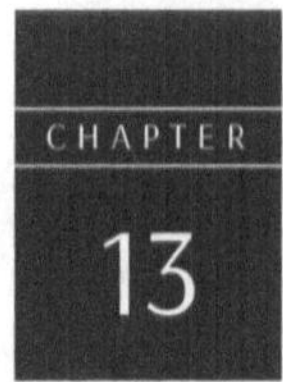

CONCLUSION

This book can't encapsulate everything you will face in your day-to-day work. The job is too varied. A constantly evolving workday is what I love most about post production, and I hope you'll find it exciting too. You'll learn a lot on the job. I've given you a basic breakdown of your duties and some solid tips, but the best way to be good at something is to go out and do it.

Post production assistant work is vital to the film industry and a great way to begin your post production career. Keep your resume updated and crisp. Search for work confidently. Stay polite and upbeat. Bring a notebook. Work hard at every task. Make great connections. Learn as much as you can, and above all, stick with it.

This industry needs your creativity and hard work.

Keep going.

SUGGESTED ADDITIONAL
READING

The TV-AE Blog at www.tv-ae.com/blog

TV-AE's Curated Book Lists at www.tv-ae.com/resources

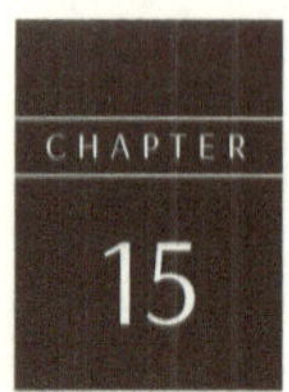

CHAPTER

15

WORKS CITED

Aaker, Jennifer Lynn, and Naomi Bagdonas. *Humor, Seriously: Why Humor Is a Secret Weapon in Business and Life and How Anyone Can Harness It. Even You.* Currency, 2021.

"12.0 Acceptable Documents for Verifying Employment Authorization and Identity." *USCIS*, 20 May 2022, www.uscis.gov/i-9-central/form-i-9-resources/handbook-for-employers-m-274/120-acceptable-documents-for-verifying-employment-authorization-and-identity.

Gómez-Pinilla, Fernando. "Brain foods: the effects of nutrients on brain function." Nature reviews. Neuroscience vol. 9,7 (2008): 568-78. doi:10.1038/nrn2421.

Duckworth, Angela. *Website FAQ's - What is Grit?* https://angeladuckworth.com/qa.

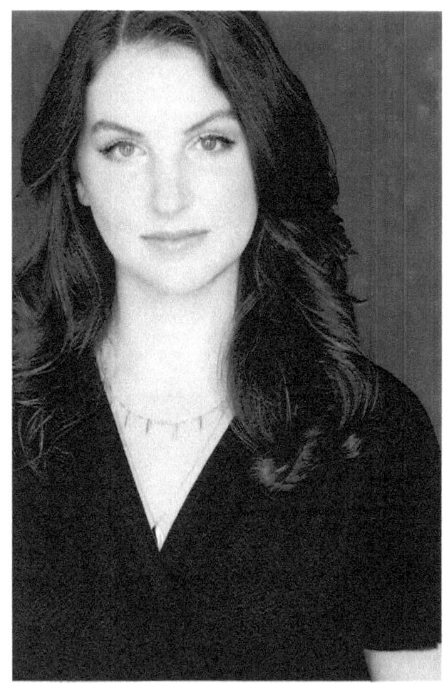

Photo Credit: Stephanie Girard
Photography

About the Author

Alyssa Carroll is a television editor and the creator of TV-AE.com. At the beginning of her career she yearned for detailed books and on-line tutorials to help her enhance her workplace performance. Now, after more than a decade in the film and television industry, Alyssa has dedicated herself to creating those resources for future post production professionals.